THE KNOPF POETRY SERIES

1   Robert Mazzocco, *Trader*
2   Cynthia Macdonald, *(W)holes*
3   Thomas Rabbitt, *The Booth Interstate*
4   Edward Hirsch, *For the Sleepwalkers*
5   Marie Ponsot, *Admit Impediment*
6   Brad Leithauser, *Hundreds of Fireflies*
7   Katha Pollitt, *Antarctic Traveller*
8   Nicholas Christopher, *On Tour with Rita*
9   Amy Clampitt, *The Kingfisher*
10 Alan Williamson, *Presence*
11 Stephen Sandy, *Riding to Greylock*
12 Pamela White Hadas, *Beside Herself*
13 Sharon Olds, *The Dead and the Living*
14 Peter Klappert, *The Idiot Princess of the Last Dynasty*
15 Mary Jo Salter, *Henry Purcell in Japan*
16 Norman Williams, *The Unlovely Child*
17 Marilyn Hacker, *Assumptions*
18 Amy Clampitt, *What the Light Was Like*
19 Cynthia Macdonald, *Alternate Means of Transport*
20 Brad Leithauser, *Cats of the Temple*
21 Edward Hirsch, *Wild Gratitude*
22 Brooks Haxton, *Dominion*

Dominion

Dominion

poems by
Brooks Haxton

Alfred A. Knopf   New York   1986

THIS IS A BORZOI BOOK
PUBLISHED BY ALFRED A. KNOPF, INC.

Some of the poems in this book appeared previously in the following:
American Poetry Review, "Justice"; *Beloit Poetry Journal*, "Economics,"
"Glee," "What Would Make a Boy Think to Kill Bats?"; *Chicago Review*,
"Peaceable Kingdom," "Not Wild or Mongolian Now, nor Ever Truly an Ass,"
"The Clarinet"; *Poetry*, "Breakfast ex Animo," "Bones," "Tongue," "Hand and
Foot"; *The Southern Review*, "Easter Mass for Little John," "Los Angeles,"
"Serenade Airborne"; *Tendril*, "Recess," "The Conversion Shift," "I Live
to See Strom Thurmond Head the Judiciary Committee," "Anthropology,"
"The Excellence of a Good Breakfast," "Witness"; *Monitor Anthology*, 1984,
"Tongue."

Library of Congress Cataloging-in-Publication Data

Haxton, Brooks
   Dominion : poems.
   I. Title.
PS3558.A825D6 1986   811'.54   85-45777
ISBN 0-394-55062-5
ISBN 0-394-74295-8 (pbk.)

Manufactured in the United States of America
First Edition

for my parents

Acknowledgments

Lewis P. Simpson gave me a start by publishing poems of mine in *The Southern Review* before any had been published elsewhere, and by publishing my first long poem. John Frederick Nims kept me going by publishing my second long poem in *Poetry*. Syracuse University supported me with a University Fellowship while I was writing several of the shorter poems here. Thanks also to my friends and family for their support and—especially to Philip Booth, Hayden Carruth, Gail Irish, Anthony Robbins, and above all to my wife, Francie—for their persistent help in revision.

Contents

I

Breakfast ex Animo   3

II

Justice   21
Recess   24
I Live to See Strom Thurmond Head
    the Judiciary Committee   26
The Conversion Shift   28
Anthropology   30
Los Angeles   33
The Excellence of a Good Breakfast   36

III

Still Life with Fruit, 1969, Missing in Action   41
Beans   42
Witness   44
Leaving the Drugstore for Example   46
Serenade Airborne   47
Walking Home in the Dark   53
Anatomy   55

IV

Easter Mass for Little John   67

V

What Would Make a Boy Think to Kill Bats?   87
Peaceable Kingdom   89
Economics   90
Glee   91
Hand and Foot   94
Not Wild or Mongolian Now, nor
     Ever Truly an Ass   95
The Clarinet   97
Pond   98

Notes   105

Thou madest him to have dominion over the works
of thy hands; thou hast put all things under his feet:
All sheep and oxen, yea, and the beasts of the
field;
The fowl of the air, and the fish of the sea, and
whatsoever passeth through the paths of the seas.

Psalms 8:6–8

I'm truly sorry man's dominion
Has broken Nature's social union,
An' justifies that ill opinion
        Which makes thee startle
At me, thy poor earth-born companion,
        An' fellow-mortal!

"To a Mouse: on Turning Her Up
in Her Nest with the Plough,
November, 1785" by Robert Burns

Dominion

I

Breakfast ex Animo

The red-tailed hawk perched in the toothache tree by the front porch
Faces me over morning coffee.
Three deer sail through the back row of sweet corn,
Clear the top strand of barbed wire,
Take five quick bounds apiece in the dewberry briars,
And break into the dark woods each with two flicks of her tail.
The coons retire from their crimes at the hint of dawn,
Still there is one dragging a cornstalk through the fence backwards
With both hands.
On the powerline two doves coo aloud, chortle to themselves,
And resume necking.
Venus rises.
The armadillo that lives under the woodpile
Cruises the Jerusalem artichokes for tubers.
"I'm helpless before coffee," I confess to the hawk,
Who recalls,
Miles down, on some hillside,
Some fool avenging himself on nature
With his pump-action twelve-gauge,
Me.
Taking flight with a pounce towards me,
She veers low into the close growth of the gulley
With slow strokes
Maneuvering
Through thickets where no bird that big could fly
While one aerodynamically unfeasible housefly

Dive-bombs my scrambled eggs.
Aurora,
Readying herself in the black treetops,
Releases her long waves of light
In the limpid ultramarine
Like a red laden brushtip touched to one edge of a wet page
And the cock goes crazy.
Can't the frizzly rooster announce dawn to the frizzly hen
Without heralding doomsday
Or the shambles?
"So much, doves, for the bucolic breakfast,"
I nod, grabbing my cane
As I round the corner for the henhouse,
Where,
According to the rooster,
Snakes, foxes, nutrias, and opossums contend,
And the catamount routs all for the spoils,
But the catamount,
Alias bobcat, alias painter, screaming painter, alias lynx,
Whether in ectoplasm or the flesh,
Rarely shows his small, sleek, whiskery, malignant head,
Although one centenarian neighbor of mine,
Henry Davis,
On sleepless nights the final five years of his life,
Could hear, far off, a painter scream
In the old peach grove near Second Creek

Where his and his first wife's house used to stand,
And where their twelve—sometimes he said twenty—
Children were born.
Back at the obstreperous henhouse,
I spot atop the gatepost
A Komodo dragon-like lizard, three inches long,
And he spots me.
He does eight rapid push-ups while his neck puffs out
Until a pink madras coin protrudes under his chin.
The staccato puck puck puck scream
Keeps repeating itself inside the tiny coop
While outside,
Having latched the gate,
I stand still,
Bois d'arc cane in my right hand,
Momentarily to collect my wits.
No, I am not awake.
I come barefoot, prepared to meet a rattlesnake,
Ready to beat mama possum with a cane,
When any numbskull would have boots on and a gun.
Wait.
The weathered, guttered, knotty, foot-wide
Cypress planks of the henhouse,
Streaked before sunrise with dew,
Might well admit a snake,
A small nutria, not to starve,

Could claw, gnaw, scuttle, and squeeze in,
But no possum, I'll assume, and doubtless not the lynx.
The chickenyard scent of guano and dust soaked with dew rises
While all Earth is still,
Wind, pond water, dark woods,
Cloudless blue, green, rose depth in the East,
All still,
Except, inside the carpentered box, behind the rustic wooden latch,
The puck puck puck scream and loud beating of clipped wings
Invisibly made by the frizzly rooster with horrific regularity
As by the works of an apocalyptic metronome.
The frizzly hen looked fine last night,
Hypnotized,
When I lifted her to add four eggs to half-a-dozen she had laid.
Six days ago I put the porcelain doorknob in her nest,
Imperishable egg, to make her set,
And she, obediently fecund, far, albeit, from intelligent, complied.
Now while I turn the latch and while the frizzly rooster evokes
Erebus, Nemesis, Nyx, and all their cohorts,
The dire demiurges of the dark,
I conjure scenes of mayhem:
Friz, her saucy, tousled head
Drooped on the near rim of the nest,
The mangled neck,
Her viscera depending from an open side
Upon the doorknob and remains of eggs,

While her assassin,
Valuable pelt all caked with slime,
The nutria—to an Araucan, coypu, here, the devil rat—
Springs effortlessly from her nest
To scurry,
A tight squeeze,
Out the same hole where he weaseled in.
But nutrias don't eat eggs,
Much less kill hens.
I crack the door,
And while the rooster screams his head off
I deliberate.
The striking range of the pit viper—
Whose heat-sensitive pits,
Behind the eyes,
By now would have detected my warmth
On the far side of the door—
The striking range, I say, of this pit viper—
Whether moccasin or rattlesnake—
Equals the extension of the letter S suspended in the upheld neck
Or one third the spine's length from head to tail.
The longest rattler I've seen had twelve rattles
And he measured more than six feet,
A foot longer than myself at that time
When we hunted rats in the same barn.
The morning we met I took aim

And blew the knothole out between his eyes
With one puff of long rifle rat shot.
Now, to that snake's equal, coiled on Friz's nest,
An eyeball at the crack of this door
Is no kindred creature
But a target,
As the apparition of the head's wedge was to me,
Reared,
One yard from my knee,
The flickering, olfactory tongue tasting my flesh
In the calm heat,
Each brow bone, arch for an obsidian pebble set in gold,
When an unearthly trill
Ascended
From the shaken tail
On freezing spiral tracks around my spine.
I tear open the door
And the frizzly rooster barrels past my leg into the yard crying,
"PAHCK puck puck puck puck puck
PAHCK puck puck puck puck
PAHCK puck puck
PAHCK puck puck puck."
He runs and his head bobs
While his legs volley his speeding bulk around the yard,
Wings flapped for balance,
And his holding pattern looks like the collision course of an electron

In the wrong shell,
But I can't be bothered,
Because—
Though with Friz frozen
On the head of the snake
I can't tell which kind,
Diamondback rattlesnake, or gray rat snake, or copperhead—
I know
That the jaw,
Having unhinged itself,
Is at work to swallow or let go of that last egg
So he can leave,
Because snakes listen for vibrations,
And he,
His belly's auditory membrane to the ground,
Has known
Since I first twisted the latch
That I am here.
Friz cocks her unkempt, characteristic frizzly's head,
Not stirring feather one below the neck,
And catches me with a quick beaded look
That says,
"Hold it, peabrain
If this son of a bitch is deadly
The one dead will be me,"
And her gaze plunges

Like that of some frizzly prophet
Surveying
From Moab
Judah to the utmost sea.
What's visible,
With drab chains of geometry draped down its length,
Too red to be a rattlesnake,
The wrong shade for a copperhead,
Too fat to be a copperhead too,
I'm nearly certain,
Is a gray rat snake,
Although a copperhead could be that fat
Pregnant,
She, the most treacherous of the pit vipers,
Being the unsnake-like one
Who bears an already poisonous brood of six alive.
I feel certain that it is a gray rat snake,
Yet while heaven goes red
On a blue field etched with small violet clouds,
Though nearly certain,
I still wait
Until I see the head.
Friz meanwhile seems to have attained satori,
Or at least the sorrowful, rapt look
Mary gives
In the annunciations

Where she's said to have foreseen the Passion,
Which leaves me as an annunciating angel
Flourishing a bois d'arc wand for lilies,
And the snake, apparently, must be the dove.
The rooster's quiet outside
And the customary doves call.
Miles off
An early lumber truck winds down toward first gear
On Springfield Hill.
Inside an east-facing henhouse blanched cypress boards redden.
I begin to doubt
My savoir faire with snakes,
Because this one has had time to drop egg
And haul ass
And here he is.
I pin his back with one end of the bois d'arc wand
And simultaneously
Out of nest and shadow
Emerge head and anfractuous tail,
Fangless, without rattles,
To investigate and wrest off the cane.
I can relax.
Even when he rears to strike
And vibrates his tailtip
Between dry cypress boards,
Aping his more musical cousin,

Even though he must be five feet long,
I know
That he's all show
And when I reach to take hold of his neck
He wallops into my left thumb so hard
The impact jars my hand,
And he hangs on.
In criminal code
Assault is the mere threat
And battery, the beating,
But to be hypnotized and bitten
Before breakfast
By enormous
(Even nonpoisonous)
Snakes
Is no crime
But a nightmare.
In the nightmare,
While the yawning head glides
Toward my knuckle
An officious, cosmopolitan agent in the brain
Transmits, without authority,
Alarming messages
To the incredulous, provincial muscles of the thumb.
"Out of the way, boys. Withdraw. Watch out now! Dodge! It's . . ."
The gray rat snake,

Here in his capacity as chicken snake,
Having acted in a tour de force
As thumb snake,
Writhes off the cane,
Lets my thumb go,
And heads out the knothole beside Friz's nest,
Not hurriedly,
Nor with malevolent phlegm,
Like the pit viper,
But with fluid and exact economy
Until the swallowed egg a foot behind his head sticks.
On both sides of my knuckle
Horseshoe-shaped rows of toothpricks
Leak like the riddles from six dozen lancets
Until red drops drop from my thumbtip
Onto the red tinted dust floor.
Day breaks.
Phoebus squeaks by the horizon.
The snake battles in vain to break the swallowed egg,
In vain
Because the egg is not an egg,
Is nothing to be swallowed,
Is
The antique porcelain doorknob from Friz's nest.
Below the flattened ovoid bulge
The metal stem stands out,

Drawing the cream-colored skin of the belly so taut
That scales bend,
Separate,
And the convexity
At the rounded head of a small subcutaneous screw
Shows.
Darwin would have deemed this feeding pattern
Maladaptive,
Hence unlikely to enhance the species,
Save by proving fatal,
Thus removing feeble genes from the genetic pool.
Failed long since as a naturalist,
I learn
That the henhouse I built in the wilderness
Is not less
Than Plato's Cave,
And the oblivious serpent therein eats the bogus egg
Only to find his way prevented
By the very implement of release.
My thumb smarts, still I feel profound.
The snake looks unenlightened though,
And who knows
How callus-, fur-, and talon-eating enzymes
Handle doorknobs, if at all?
The four-foot rope of unavailing muscle writhes,
And when I grab the knob in my right hand

The body, looping my wrist,
Spirals up my forearm
Like a bullwhip
Wrapping itself around a post.
Pressing the knob to the knothole
So the head can't come inside,
While cool, peristaltic ripples fill my palm,
And coils tightening on my forearm
Call to mind
The reputation of the rat snake as constrictor,
I begin to smell
The newly released smear of musk
Fortified with guano
Lacing the air.
Day is full-fledged.
Clear light strikes the bleeding thumb
From which a warm drop plummets
Onto the bare, sensitive ramp of the left foot.
I tug the knob,
But the snake latches himself on the far side of the board
And the scales
Caught in the cypress's grain
Tear with a dry whisper.
I try twisting the knob
And the snake comes unlatched
By what looks like a mechanical function

Absorbed from the doorknob's former life, as,
In one groundbreaking experiment,
Worms "learned"
The reticulum of an unfamiliar maze
By eating other worms
That had learned first hand,
Or
As the reader of a poem
May be said to learn
The arcanum of the gray rat snake at dawn
Without bothering to acquire
The bitten thumb.
I pin the head now with the cane in my left hand
And take hold of the neck.
Friz,
Who has kept put,
Angling her gaze with pert accuracy,
Watches me back out,
Snake upheld in the wilderness,
And begins shifting her eggs
For an even seat.
Summer leaves and grassblades revel
In the early light
To the revival music of an insect orchestra
Performing the most recent overture
To their serenade.

Traffic picks up on the Liberty Road.
In the spirit of things
I go down through the woods
Past flower- and thorn-bearing vines
Into the dark tangle of choked weeds
To celebrate
The ceremonial release of the gray rat snake at dawn,
And on the clay floor where the shadows are,
Where the cool mist hangs,
I leave him,
Motionless and alert.
He could die.
He could come back.
He could learn
Never to steal eggs from a frizzly hen.
And the doorknob, like Jonah
When God took pity on him and Nineveh,
Could be found in mullein
Near dewberry bushes in bloom, or purpled with sweet fruit,
By some untraveled cowpath,
Probably not.
Probably,
When I get back to the front porch,
One fly
Will be sampling the congealed grease on my scrambled eggs,
And the armadillo that lives under the woodpile

Will be sleeping.
The doves will have alighted elsewhere,
And the coon, gone.
Venus will have slipped into the blue folds of translucent sky,
And I will find myself at breakfast,
And begin.

I I

I have laid in the jail with my face turned to the wall
I have laid in the jail with my face turned to the wall
It was doctors and lawyers says son you the cause of it all

"Unhappy Blues," by Walter Vinson
of The Mississippi Sheiks

Justice

I'll have to look up the name of the son of a bitch
Who tried to pick that fight in the locker room
With James Cole. James was a skinny black kid—
Half-pint smart-ass, like me—and we were friends
In a friendship that had to be complex
Since he was one of the first few black kids

In the all-white schools. Sometimes in homeroom,
Which was Chemistry Lab, we'd share a table
And snide remarks, and if some people thought
We were laughing at their expense, that was
Because we were. I remember a girl
From Teen Club came to collect donations

For the Homecoming Dance. I asked her, nodding
Toward James, were they keeping the niggers out.
She was embarrassed to say, and I
Was never again invited to Teen Club
Affairs, not even my own Graduation Dance,
Which I considered an honor not to attend.

James was getting dressed out, joking with me,
When the kid whose name I've forgotten said,
"You think you're hot shit." "No, man, I don't think
I'm any kind of shit, I swear." James wanted

To turn it into a joke, but he failed.
"I'd say you're shit." This almost syllogistical

Repartee was interrupted by Malcolm
Davis, with whom any life-loving redneck
Would not want to fuck. Yet Malcolm, though angry—
And he was losing his patience in general—
Kept his voice calm: "White trash," the locker room
Got quiet as catacombs, and Malcolm

And James were the only two black kids around,
"Why would you pick a fight with James here seeing
As James is so much smaller than you? Couldn't be
You're a coward, could it? A . . . peckerwood
Coward? I'm your size. You're not picking a fight
With me. Why is that, white trash? Might get hurt?

"Look. I put my hands behind my back, OK?
Now, you want to hit somebody, hit me."
What's-his-name, who seemed to have lost that sense
Of an imperative vengeance devolving
On him, now stammered excuses, backed off.
How did you get away with it, Malcolm,

Not to get away with it after all?
Was it three years later I saw you, saw

On the *Delta Democrat Times'* front page
After sentencing for armed robbery,
Fist overhead, your face? Manslaughter, was it?
The clerk at the Chinese grocery store died,

Or . . . ? Forget it, Malcolm. I can look it up.

Recess

I feel it now, that rage I felt at seven,
The time I wanted revenge on Larry Ables.
What did he do? I can remember only
My rage stalking the second-grade playground,
Clenching my fists to summon up the picture
Of Larry Ables in full repugnant detail.

He wasn't a bad-looking kid, not even
Detestably handsome. Tall and freckled,
Red-headed, with new jeans and a plaid shirt—
Country come to town, polite and shy.
Still I remember my fury, clenching
And unclenching my fists, furious with myself

For not knowing where I should hold my thumbs
When I punched him. That was it. With myself.
Larry might not have known he had done anything.
He kept playing freeze tag while I stalked.
And what could I do now? I didn't want
To hurt him or be hurt. I was afraid

Of how I felt, afraid to break the rules,
Afraid to call attention to myself,
Afraid what Mrs. Rowell would say, what
Other kids would think. I didn't want to care!

And my rage was as enormous and as painful
Even as fear. I tightened my lips

And told myself I would act in so daring,
So just, and so effective a way that no one
Would challenge my seven-year-old independence
Ever again. Not ever! Never! The bell
At the end of recess rang, and I stood
Under Mrs. Rowell's right hand, first in line.

I Live to See Strom Thurmond
Head the Judiciary Committee

Greenville rhymes with "teenful" in the native speech.
I belonged to the Teen Club there one year.
The Teen Club had been formed to keep school dances
White now that the schools were two percent
Desegregated. I knew that. I knew
It was inexcusable to belong,

But dances were the best place to take girls,
Still I hated the dances, and I quit.
At the Klan rally outside town one night,
Shelton, Grand Imperial Wizard, spoke.
I was there with integrationist friends.
We didn't call attention to ourselves,

But watched them burn a fifteen-foot-high cross
Wrapped in burlap and doused with gasoline.
There were women and children there in hoods
Picnicking under the flames, and smoke you could taste.
Shelton said that seven Jews in New York—
Who ran the world—had been sending firearms

To the Catholic priests in the South. Yeah,
The Catholics stored them all in the basements
Of churches, and then the beatniks and SNCC-
Working communists came to give the word

To the niggers to pick up their guns, and,
Brothers and sisters, in sweet Jesus' name,

Will you be there to stop that massacre
Now that we know the truth? Flames on the cross
Were dying along its arms, when somebody
Snipped the powerline to the stage, and the lights
And the mikes and speakers went dead, and people
Held guns in the dark when it started to rain.

The Conversion Shift

After he'd had the Hurst Conversion Shift
Put into our parents' Buick Special,
Ayres and his friend Dwight took Louis and me
Snake hunting one day on Old Warfield Road
Where the barrow pits were a garden for water snakes
And the road had a good quarter-mile strip marked off.

We'd been looking to catch a mud snake,
The red and yellow pattern on whose belly
Made it our most brilliantly marked species.
Having caught, though mud galore, no snake,
Louis, Dwight, and I were muddy enough
We couldn't ride in the car, so we perched

On the trunk lid, banked at an awful pitch,
With no toe-hold, and no hand-hold, and Ayres
Set about taking her through the gears. I sat
By Dwight, my redneck bodyguard from rednecks
Who would have been happy to pound the shit
Out of a nigger-lover like me, but knew Dwight,

Unlike me, weren't no nigger-lover and
Fought back. At the lunge into second gear
When I started to slide down losing my grip
On the chrome trim of the rear window, I

Asked Dwight, did he have a good hold? He said,
"No!" through clenched teeth. There was no question about it.

I was gliding down slowly away, hands
Slipping with mud to smear the coppery
Finish when we lunged into third. At what?
Ayres said the optimum speed for the shift
Into third was around fifty. Therefore,
At an optimum speed of, say, fifty or more,

I was about to touch down, backflip down
Old Warfield Road in hysterical fear.
Dwight watched my skidding hands accelerate
Into frenzy. Looks met one last time.
With what blue eyes love nearly threatening
Eked out my poor courage to say goodbye!

Anthropology

In the fall of 1969, I read
Village in Vietnam in Anthro
101. I didn't like the book much
More than anything I did in school. What
Interested me that fall was Bobby Gates.
We went camping up north and fell in love.

We had a double sleeping bag. The second
Night, when I took her clothes off, she said, "Why
Didn't we do this last night?" and I laughed.
Her body was more beautiful to me
Than anything I could imagine, even
With the fire low, where we couldn't see.

We were up all night. It's embarrassing
How inept I was. She was a virgin—
I was an ignoramus—still at dawn.
Had daylight ever been that good to me?
Christmas, maybe, when I was four years old?
Bobby lying there, buck naked, glad she was,

With faint light's coming on till she took shape.
Why does a seventeen-year-old slight girl

Still have such power over a thirty-
Year-old man? I was eighteen then, and I
Had never seen a girl look happier
To have been undressed and made much of by me.

For the next two months, we fooled around,
Till she got bored with it, not just the sex,
Mostly, though, the sex. I figured that, since
She'd been a virgin, she would have to make
The physical adjustment, which takes time.
I, meanwhile, didn't know where her clit was.

Anyway, she left. Then, I left for Thanksgiving.
I hadn't seen one brother since high school.
He'd been stationed outside Bangkok for two years.
To leave he had to break up with a woman
He'd been living with, a Thai, who hired someone
To put a spell on him. It didn't work.

I went back to college for my exams.
Deborah, a friend of mine from high school, came
To visit shortly before the final
In Anthro. She was in love with me.

She thought we would be getting married soon,
But she knew better than to mention it.

I knew Deborah had this crush, but not how bad.
I wanted to talk about Bobby Gates.
Deborah said I should study for my test.
I said I hadn't gone to class for weeks.
What was the point? I'd flunk. Then, half an hour
Before the final started, Bobby showed up.

Deborah excused herself while Bobby and I talked.
This was a goodbye visit. She gave me
A potted plant, bright red, with stickers at
The leaftips about which she had done nothing
To warn me when she held it out. "Shit, girl!
This thing could hurt somebody," I said. She said—

She had a very childlike smile, "I know."

Los Angeles

Somebody set fire to my brother's house.
He came home from a movie and fire trucks were there.
The fire had been set under my visiting
Mother's bed. Everything she'd had with her
Was gone: a suitcase full of clothes, a book
She had been writing about middle age.

She found the metal rim of a briefcase
She had bought for traveling, never to let
The manuscript into strangers' hands. She picked
The rim out of a wet pile of ashes, only
The rim, the rim shut, latched. She took it,
Opened it. The latches and the hinges worked.

My brother thought the wiring must have shorted—
Sparks dropped in the wall and kindled. That day,
Though, two houses up, another fire charred
Someone's back wall without catching. Were the choices
Random? Is it a pointless perversion,
And violence to the imagination,

To imagine who—in what condition,
What sick human animal—had crept
Into my brother's house that afternoon
To make his fire under my mother's bed

And burn the book she thought would be worth years,
Irrecoverable years of her one life?

May be. But when I do imagine him,
I think of him in the rapture of striking the match,
Letting the red-blue spurt from nowhere
Into the room. Roberto, next door, when
He heard the fire, thought it was water running
And came round to turn it off. Is this the saddest

Part of the story? Roberto, who loves Richard—
I think, thwartedly desires him, and has
Loved him, suffering to be his friend, for years—
When he discovered the fire, thought Richard
Was inside. He stood at the kitchen door.
The flames were at the far end of the house.

But the air in the kitchen was sufficient
To be melting plastic bottlecaps and knobs
On the appliances. He opened the door
Thinking the one he loved could be inside
And his body irresistibly leapt back
For shelter, cringed, would not go in. Still,

He called. He called and called my brother's name.
"Reechard!" His pain was indescribable,

His fear of something human in the smoke.
Richard came home to fire trucks that night, and men,
And vague smoldering possessions thrown out
Into the dark yard. The next morning Mama

Located the metal rim of her briefcase.
Having gotten this much of the story,
You have to know about the house, that it was
Adequately insured; about Roberto,
That he has had lovers all the time that he
And Richard have been friends; and—what's amazing—

About the manuscript in the wet ashes,
That they found it in three separate stacks, complete,
With margins eaten away by fire, yet
None of it illegible. One more thing:
A retired black couple from across the street
Came over that next morning and without

Belaboring the point gave Richard two tens and a five.

The Excellence of a Good Breakfast

Francie, you know the last love poem I wrote
Was a goodbye forever—it was to you—
And we've had several goodbyes forever since,
Goodbyes between us, and with others too,
But we're still sleeping in the homemade bed
With Salvation Army mattress from '75.

Now you're ready to have a kid, I'm not,
And understandably we fight; or now
It's understandable: then, nobody cares.
We curse each other; you sulk; and I throw things,
Inexpensive things that I can break.
Maybe we'll hate each other for a month.

Maybe forgive each other before long:
Make love that night, unable to tell tears
Of joy from tears of helplessness. However
It goes, we wonder what it means. Are we
Mismatched, unkind, or just mismanaging?
How much can we expect to know in love?

Or is it love to make things go so wrong?
Lately it's been easier to be good

And we lie down nights in each other's arms.
Yesterday for breakfast we had trout, smoked,
Bagels, and soft cheese. Am I changing the subject?
It was the best breakfast I believe I've had.

III

I am dry with thirst and am dying. Give me then quickly
the water that runs cold out of the lake of Memory.

Inscription on gold leaf found in a tomb
from the 7th century BC, translated from
the Greek by Richmond Lattimore

Still Life with Fruit, 1969,
Missing in Action

Imagine, smaller than a mayfly's wing,
His right hand, mirrored
Palm up, empty, fingers curled
As though remembering
An apple, or a peach.

Folded forever triple
In an envelope folded double
Under the pocket flap snapped shut
By the chrome snap reflecting the hand,
Over his heart, the letter starting,
"I saw D. at the liquor store.
He told me where you were."

But no telling where now,
Holding under the mirror,
As in offering,
That nameless fruit,
Unable to let go.

Beans

Three beans' worth of the brew in my coffee cup
Came from an equatorial mountainside
Down which the man whose hand had plucked them fell.
Cold sweat formed in his face. His world-consuming
Agony enacted on a green slope
Under high frail ribcages of clouds
In the dispassionate sunlight made pain look
Like an ecstasy, except that now he puked
Over the burlap bag full of raw beans,
Clutching it as a child with nightmares might
His pillow, and he puked again, and, less, again,
Until he came up empty, and the light froth
Shaken by his breath lay glistering in the dirt.
His cousin kneeled and called three cousins' names,
Each of whom now took one twitching limb,
And lifted him who was about to die.
The foreman kicked the vomit off the bag,
And frowned, and coughed, following bag in hand
The five, by now four, cousins into camp.
He had made a mistake. But who would have thought
To let a man stop spraying would not be enough?
Who would have given a man like that time off?
A man like that would just have died in camp.

A man like that, unlike Americans big
In coffee, in chemical, and in shipping concerns,
Unlike the foreman, unlike me at my desk
Drinking this cup of poison without tears.

Witness

Succor, Surcease, Comfort,
None, no human animal can endure without,
Thou Source and Cause, Thou Agent, Purpose,
Unrevealed one numerous Nature,
World-, idea-, mind-containing—
Thee I summon from inside Thine Own
Inconstant, constant Being:

       Engle Washington,
Who tended cattle not for profit—
But he would have told You if You'd asked him,
"I just loves the country, ain't no money in it"—

Why should Engle have been taken
             By the auger
         Of an oil rig,
            By the pants cuff
        Have been taken,
             To be spun into the hole
        And twisted, spiraled
             By the blade down his whole
        Body till, too late,

They had switched off the motor
And his head lay at the bore's lip

And, too late, they could stand looking
Into Engle's face and wonder
From that dead man's
Swollen incommunicative grimace
What—exactly—happened
To the small and energetic capable man's body—

Give me not this day
Thy Kingdom. Nor Thy Will
Be done. Let
Quasar unto quasar,
Turning back, tear
With such Mercy
Up Thine Unrepentant Ass,
Thou Infinite Begetter
Of all finitudes and endings.

Leaving the Drugstore for Example

The small bag bursts into flame in his hands.
His thin hair smokes while the aerosol can
At his bosom bulges until it explodes
Hairspray ignited into his melting face.
Half the planet is dark with cities on fire
At night, and half the planet, light, with cities
Burning by day. Now having lit the world
With hellfire the elders could hardly imagine,
Now while the touch of sunlight blisters the cheek,
When dead fish and dead shorebirds litter the shore,
Left to our own devices, none of us
Needs to believe in Hell. No one need believe.

Serenade Airborne

The Desert Going Under

Butte, mesa, arroyo, badlands, flatlands,
Wide and narrow winding bands of earth tone,
Red and yellow, brown and golden, bone white,
Naked substance of the planet turning east
Toward shadow into the night, into the conical
Shadow with vague tip sweeping, indicating
A path of light through darkness, invisible
Shadow under the arrowtip of the clock's hand,
And the clock has no face, makes no sound. The plane
Hums. The body—pump-pump pump-pump—is pumping.

The body cannot conceive of this location.

Intelligence can conceive of a metal ship
Afloat in the jet stream over a mountain
Where hundreds of us ranked like oarslaves pull
On Diet Cokes, on cocktails. Intelligence
Can make this unimpressive, or it can open
The plastic eyelid and the mind fall
Into amazement.

                Lo! Lower thine eyes
Unto the hills from whence cometh thy help.

Thy help cometh from Lockheed which made
Not heaven but hull and wing and tailfin.

The metal wants to go back into the mountain.
The mountain yearns up after the stolen metal.
The moon at four o'clock, first quarter, yearns
For the metal, the mountain. The body yearns
For the faint moon faintly. Having set foot
On the moon the body has altered in yearning.
For the moon is altered. The moon is another place,
More like Cincinnati, only farther away,
Without a ball park. The moon is traveling
East among the stars which are fixed. The mind
Has put them in constellations. The fixed stars
Travel at speeds the body cannot conceive of.
The body travels (at speeds the body
Cannot conceive of) toward Los Angeles.

The Point of Departure

And angels are no more among the clouds.
The body is among the clouds. The troops
Of living bodies move in the clouds. Yea!
The celestial company rises. Behold!

And on what errand? They rise. Is it love?

Their craft worldwide on metal wings have risen.
Toward Quang Ngai, toward Beirut, toward Dresden, toward where
We have sped them on their errand.

                              That errand again,
What was it? What did we say was the errand?

The Blackout

Somebody was in Times Square in a taxi
And the meter was running. Something went wrong
In Times Square and in every part of the City.
The City collapsed in a shadow, dead,
No lights now but headlights, still the meter
Was running. Enormous, intricate hardware,
Messages, towers, trains in their tunnels, went dead,
And the meter was running. The taxi's engine
Was running. The body itself was running.
Therefore, celebration. Wine and cheese and candles
Down on the street in the Village. Looting and fire
In Harlem. A mood of celebration. How
It must have looked from the air! New York City
Blown out. Little waves of darkness lapping
Over the lights of Manhattan, each, and after
Nothing.

The Point of Arrival

      Passengers look frightened yet
They seem not to notice. Los Angeles
Flight control prevents traffic from colliding.
Elsewhere, under remote mountains, the computers
Fret about the destruction, calculate
The logic of ending civilization.
To the ninth decimal place can that circuitry
Quantify Armageddon. With a few minutes'
Margin of error, prophesy Golgotha,

Hinnom, habitation laid waste burning,
Waters, winds, and earth to inherit, desert,
Fire in the earth, fire of the stars to inherit,
Darkness inherit fire, and fire be dark.

The Gate

St. Francis in the Frick stands calm outside
His cavern, preparing to receive stigmata,
Looking up into the air as into the Spirit
Descending. Eight hundred years ago he could hear,
Closing on him, the guided missile. Goodbye,
Francis. The plane has arrived at its gate.
Attendants and passengers say goodbye
Without meaning it. Ciao, everybody! Farewell!
Is our mind not made? Have we not decided?
The Powers among themselves have decided: time
Has come that we leave. Nothing but silliness
Here, among the computers and warheads, even
To ask forgiveness, even to say goodbye.

Walking Home in the Dark

Across the enormity of the doomed
Universe last night under the doomed trees
Doomed in expiring moonlight on cracked sidewalks
Worn by wearing this doomed pair of boots,
I walked the mile between my job and home
Toward certain yet not only toward but from
And through and into certain what? well, doom,
Walked in early dark in early autumn
Early into manhood walked home late from work
Among the summer's worth of dismissed leaves
Turned brown, left broken, drowned, and trampled,
Driven-over pride of summer, walked
In this green body aging my way home
Past houses renovated or in ill repair
And thought of you my friend and our friends
Of their friendships broken by the blow
Of starlight by the season's crowbar by the moon
Dismantled, thought how friends in anger
Hurt may choose disjunction, how from disappointment
They may get them strength to be spent only
Working damage, thought of us, of our doomed love
Here among others among many walked
And thought among the walkers-home last evening
Down among the loves of many thinking walking home

How every person's thinking was an emanation
From dark earth an answer was an echo
To ferocious starlight thought think still
Of my good fortune to be doomed and walking
Moved again to turn these steps these thoughts toward home
Toward you, however dark it is, with love.

Anatomy

As then the wise Egyptians wont to lay
More on their Tombes, then houses: these of clay,
But those of brasse, or marble were: so wee
Give more unto thy Ghost, then unto thee.
                                        John Donne

Hands

They move against your body for your delight
And leave me to imagine yours for mine.
The joy they feel themselves is incomplete.
Aching under their patchwork of old scars,
Left thumb and forefinger may comb the eyebrows,
Soothing the eyelids shut, and as you breathe
My left palm on the column of your breath lifts.
Under the right your ribcage falls. They feel
What moves move us—heat lightning, quick dark,
Tilt of the night sky soaring into the blood.

Blood

It may resemble oceans, tears, or ink.
Whatever it resembles, traffic say,
Will carry that resemblance well enough
For rhetoric perhaps, but for transfusions
Blood works more like blood, which does the trick.
Hearing the breaker suck deep in the ear
Reminds me of . . . rush hour say—it's true,
But in the marrow of my bones let blood,
Whole blood, blood only, always blood, be made,
As though my say-so mattered in my bones.

Bones

Trying to imagine them behind the look
Your lover gives you, simply as one way
Toward understanding beauty's inwardness,
May fail, because the death's-head intervenes
With a dumb grin and perfectly blank stare.
Skulls house the instruments of joy in passageways
That open into thought and on the earth
At once. The dome, oblong, and otherwise
Imperfect as geometry, makes architecture
Look fastidious—this, living, keeps out rain,
Silverfish, lint, and looks serviceable,
Not grand. The husks of goat and rhino brains
Are ruggeder, but for their thickness
Ours can stand remarkable abuse.
Ribcages are resilient, durable,
And in the naked abstract after death,
Although mathematic, sinuous in design.
The skeleton of each hand and each foot
As sculpture or as engineering work
Is an improvisation on a theme
So intricate and simple, one would think,
As to be unsurpassable, yet slowly,

Slowly at work always to surpass itself.
Before they bend much most bones tend to break,
Which hurts, may cripple, and can help cause death.
The world is a hard place, and bones are hard
Enough to take so much of it so long
And nothing more. In this, they are the image
Of the very mind that they protect.
Inside them lie the sources of the blood,
Wherefrom, not from the heart, renewal comes.
Quick in their honeycomb, blood cells split
And split—away they flow toward parts unknown
With messages, food, fluid, oxygen,
Along dark capillaries, cell by cell.

Cell

If each is another world, with factories
And prefectures maintained by local law—
I am a world of worlds, a swirl of stars;
The planet is a singular living cell;
And human scale may help men cross the road
(To fetch the chicken, or retreat from tanks),
But the mind hankers after the absolute:
To unlock thought from arbitrary flesh
And take on the illimitable power,
To crack the swarm of little waves and specks.
For some such reason now, intelligence
Has trained the binding power in all things
On arbitrariness itself, on us,
And not at human peril only, but
Even to that of the living universe.

The Living Universe

Its physical dimensions are unknowable.
Earth may contain the only forms of life
Forever anywhere. The fizzling surface
Of this warm rock spinning in emptiness
Means everything if so. It means the world
In any case, which lives here only once,
Without, then with, and soon without our kinship.
Could waves break, lightnings thunder, ice form, thaw,
The clouds assume innumerable shapes,
And nothing live to notice how things change?
Only the human body can imagine
That dead image of the world. Remarkable,
In us, that this dead world has taken place,
Where is not one place for a living soul.

Soul

First, nothing inverts itself as if
In it were something to invert, as if
Such goings-on could come from nowhere,
During a lull, say, in the nonexistent
Absence of being without time and space—
Kerbang! The universe. And the soul? Well,
Maybe the generation of souls occurred
At that same juncture, beyond timelessness
Yet not quite into time, leaving the soul
Disoriented, twenty billion years now
Into the works of time, still polishing
A comeback to the original question
Of existence, whether to be or not,
And that confusion makes the soul elusive.
When light breaks into a string of prayer beads
And lead is mainly subatomic space,
Confusion makes more sense than usual.
Now matter seems no longer to exist
Except as the proportion between energy
And speed, according to which axiom
Things are themselves mere swiftness of destruction.
Intelligence converts atomic mass
As if each detonation could give more

Irrefutable proof that what we know is true.
Honey, ain't nobody knows nothing no way.
Soul tells you that. Even the honky got some soul,
And all he has to know is to be lost.
The soul the mind the body the continuum
Inextricable in and of this world
Coheres where incoherence is to die.
Saying this out loud is good. Each syllable
Lends weight, and shape, and substance to the tongue.

Tongue

Water soothes, food pleases, song delights it
And, with it, the ear. It delights itself,
Laid wet in the warm rushing air on ear-flesh,
And on love-flesh gladly will it linger,
Fluent in a language of unspoken yearning.
Dull at the tip, dull edged, and of dull color;
But by taste, by touch, keen; by articulation
Into the consonant and vowel, noun and verb,
The curse, the invocation, keen and capable
Of moving faster than we know to move it;
Patient; though resistant to the publication
Of an unkind thought, yet apt in its expression;
Untrustworthy, seduced by flavorful
And deadly toadstools for example; brave,
Foolhardy in denunciation; meek,
If not a coward, in forbearance; curious
Yet self-possessed then, singlemindedly
Apart from various possessors—stomach,
Genitals, and brain with arguable claim
Each pressing while the tongue arcs, flutters, curls
And stretches, soaks itself, runs dry, tastes,
Tingles, and goes on about what work
May, good luck holding, please itself and prosper.

IV

The king spake, and said, Belteshazzar, let not the dream,
or the interpretation thereof, trouble thee.

Daniel 4:19

Easter Mass for Little John

I

The engine of the cumulus cloud broods.
Beyond the window of the other room
Inside the dark lobe of the nimbus
Lightning flares.
Thunder groans, and rolls after the light.
Inside the unlit, wooden house
The walls and floors and ceilings,
The brain's attic
And the chambers of the heart
Are kindled, flicker, shudder.
In the vault of heaven
The placenta and the winding sheet
Rend like a burning curtain.
The imponderable moment
Wanders in the Wood of Re-enactment.
Here
It is. A white flame
Sings into a shadow,
"Path of light,
Palm-laden,
Path of the resuming dark."

2

I invoke the women in their masks,
The Muse, the mistress, the Madonna,
The disguises of time
Measured by a child,
The calendars,
The pencil marks
Inside a doorframe,
The arrival, mornings,
At the bedroom door.
Older now, I see the mask worn
Only in the veil of my departure,
And I find another woman in my house
Consoling me with her resemblance
To an early face,
And all is one,
The Telling of this story,
Or my Silence,
Each a woman, losing,
In the passion of her childbed,
The already dying body of our love.

3

Where the last rain sweeps the canopy of pines,
Under the green thatch, for miles,
In the uninterrupted shade of their own crowns,
The limbless, scaling boles
Seem to have been buried in their ranks
Like the maimed soldiers
Of an unprofitable war.
Old needles, steeped in acid,
Rust over the forest bed,
The deathbed of the seeds of everything
But the unearthly twists
Of sweet gum, their pale foliage like stars.

A Government Pine Farm neither provides home for the songbird,
Nor allows grazing land for deer,
Nor harbors the particular insect,
Nor yields fruit to the squirrel,
Nor lends ease to the mourning dove,
Nor darkens on the call note of the whippoorwill.
Its night discovers to the hawk no game
Nor prey to his more patient brother,
The unerring owl.

Wood ticks scatter on the floor.
Gnats swarm the webless corridors.
Crows roost, complaining in the limbs,
And in the thicker shadow
Night leaves in the pines,
The turkey vultures pluck the lips, the tongue, the eyes,
The testicles, the tissues housing them,
The penis and its sheath,
The asshole, and the nipples
Of a colt I lived the summer with
And murdered earlier this afternoon.

4

When I was twelve I saw John take a board to a young mare.
I saw her nostrils widen and her eyes.
And when he got his arms around her ribs and lifted her,
And flung her down on one side in the dust
And whispered from the hollow of his throat, "You shamed
    now Ruth get up,"
Once she had caught her wind and stood with her head down,
He said to me, "Look there. Sometime the Devil be with her.
But she knows right.
You gots to beat Hell out of her to make her mind."
He made Ruth mind.

But after dark his wife took up with devils
John was not the man born to beat out.
A February night toward dawn nine years ago
He drove drunk to the Gold Coast after her.
He led her from her lover's table to the car.
The Liberty Road winds from Natchez east
Between two banks of red clay
Overgrown with briars and thick weeds.
Under the deciduous trees,
Mistletoe and woodferns,
Foxfire, lichen, Spanish moss,
The headlights of John's Galaxy went tunneling toward home.
He heard the woman passed out on the back seat

Vomiting and mumbling in her sleep,
And back of her her lover,
Tailgating them at sixty in an old-model Mercury,
The cigarette fire crawling in between his lips,
Leaned on the horn. The old heap,
Weaving, nudging at the fenders and the doors, colliding,
Jolted loose the trunk-latch of John's car,
And when the lid swung open and the windshield
    blacked out at his back,
John, in his stupor, thought he had outrun the Mercury,
    and turned to look,
Leaving the Galaxy to wheel off through the briars into the
    clay bank
And catch fire while false dawn receded
From the Shepherd's vacant arms.

5

In August
The pecan trees,
Taller than the local mansions,
Draw
From the remainder underground
Of ended seasons
The investment of the dead,
Deriving from lost leaves
And fallen catkins and old limbs
The terminal buds for another spring,
Provisioning the green shelves
Toward the fall bestowal
Of the latent seed.

John, under these survivors of the storm,
The bone, a roll of pain
Wrenched in the socket of his hip,
Chose from the litter of torn limbs
One stout enough to serve him for a leg,
And made his way down slow.

6

A long cloud the shape of a fish
Arched over the northwestern horizon.
Light splashed onto its back,
Reddened and fading,
And the dark wave broke over the light.
I lay almost asleep,
The bat, the swift, the swallow
Weaving their pattern over me.
A voice came from the pond
Through the locusts and briars
Into the confusion: the circling crow,
The cricket and cicada, the chuck-will's-widow,
The wild dog, and the dove.
It seemed long after I had heard it
That the voice was gone,
Like the image of clouds
Indistinguishable
In the water where the rain is falling,
And then, slowly, while I listened,
The surface that reflected the voice
Hardened as if into glass
And the syllables of the other songs,
Ruptured on that mirror,
Flowed over the image of the voice,
And of the word, which was my name.
I thought, John is calling me.

7

I joined him down the hillside by the pond.
He said a colt, thunder-spooked in last night's storm,
Had run the cattle gap. A pain sank in my jaw.
The fetlock, brittle as pecan wood, cracked in half.
The bone lodged in the wound like a broken tooth.
And the maimed animal was Little John,
The one John promised himself he would train
For his first son, born the same Friday,
Neither one likely to be fit to ride.

8

The memory deceives us
Because what is most essential
Memory most fears, knows best,
And fails most often to remember.

A memory takes form deliberately
As the shell the serpula builds,
Intricately spiraled from the particles
Of shellfish, stone, bone, chalk,
The tower at the mouth of which he flowers,
Delicately moved as the mimosa blossom,
Poised, however, almost instantaneously,
To retract from shadows, a commotion,
Or a sudden touch:

The memory, thus, from the evidence
Of cruelty, guilt, failure, frailty, or loss
Into a shell of the cemented remnants
Of old entities now dust.

If not contemptible, coward, or suspect,
If not animal, half animal, or plant,

The memory, at least, is superstitious,
Like the tribesman on safari
Whom we saw whimper at the word
To breach a Sacred Mountain
Or explore Forbidden Caves,
Whose comical hysteria distracted him
When rocks fell, and the audience,
Led to believe Death is the fool's part,
Laughed.

In the confusion among memories
The mind succumbs
To the temptations of forgetfulness,
Remembering what soothes,
And manufacturing the memory one fears.
I cannot say what I have done
But I remember this.

That night before the storm broke
I walked out and watched
The lightning's surge fill things so
I believed
The known world was erased.
I recognized the chapter of the Quest:

The Hero, standing at the verge
Of nature's vanishing point, knowledgeable
That the Carnal Monster of Inconquerable Fear
Moves to his left,
Wheels on him
And no demon
But the colt's face
Reeled into a trace of light.
I had frightened him,
And in the dark that followed,
Hoofbeats breaking wild, the thunder,
The reminder of the real storm,
Struck and rolled.

9

John told me he tried twice to shoot the colt.
"First time I drew a bead he's steady looking at me.
He looked pitiful. Shit,
I thought I'd well as not drive in and get the vet.
He doesn't hold a prayer.
The fetlock's hanging from a strap of skin.
But I thought, shit, can't hurt to drive in.
Maybe the vet will come give him a dead shot.
Well, seems a nigger's colt don't cut it with the man.
I thought a taste of whiskey might help stand me up to it.
But no, the way that goes you wind up where you were but drunk.
Tread water till you give out. Then you drown.
Well, second time I tried it, I was sad, and him just pitiful.
I couldn't even draw a bead.
Just stood there, half an hour, looking at each other,
And the flies. Must be five hundred flies already sucking at his leg.
Cora ain't much. Blind. All she can do to watch the kids.
Hell, I ain't much myself, not since the accident.
In them lights I can't make out why she'd marry me.
Like I'll be walking up the steps sometime and burn out
    in the hip.

I can't do nothing but sit down and wait, and when I look back,
Seems I've been steady waiting: waiting to get fed, get laid,
Get married, have kids, raise them, then retire and wait
    around to die.
No, I'm not much, Brooks. Getting old. That accident's
    got me old early.
Whatcha think I do at night? Hmm? Go to sleep.
When I was your age I'd be in the back seat until dawn,
    and then get to work.
Well, anyway, I come to ask you can you shoot him,
'Cause I ain't got the stomach for it, or the nerves.''

10

The muzzle nudged between us.
I could see
The dimple flicking on the surface
Muddy the whole eye.

I looped the chain around his neck.
John drove the truck.
The body danced away,
La Danse Macabre,
Toward the shadow of the pines.

Later by the corpse,
Under the awkward fury of the wings,
I daydreamed about Hell.
Details escape me.

I can see in John's son's eye,
An eye liable to go blind before long
Like his mother's,
The mud eddy in the clear pool
Slowly, like the spiral I remember
Tearing without meaning
The faint scribble in the brain.

At dark the dead pecan tree was turned silver while the
    moon rose.
Broken only, in the stillness, by the urge to be made whole,
The fallen limbs lay spellbound in the grass,
Skeletons and hieroglyphs of longing
After loss,
And by the Constellation of the Winged Horse,
Chained fast on the rock of absence,
Where the empty wave breaks and the foam is stars,
Andromeda longed bitterly for Perseus
Who tended from the spiral course toward her
While rivers warped like wreckage under the moon.

12

At dawn
The Sisters of the Summer Triangle
Commend to us their fading attributes:
The Lyre, the Eagle, the Swan Crucified,
And we acknowledge them our own,
Awaking,
Graced with acquiescence,
To accept another music,
To bare talons,
To imagine the dual image
Of death born and birth abiding,
To speak praise,
To wonder, and to wonder
Without pausing
Until dark.

13

Morning, and the rainwater
From a clay cup
Rises into the light
Inside the earth
The rain sinking will return.
The usual star,
Constant as the energies of middle age,
The violet white hair now yellowing,
Looks to what we have left open for him:
Windows, cisterns, cradles, cracks
In the cement of highways, city lots,
The basins and the troughs
Of oceans, horsestalls, outdoor washing places,
World all one to him,
The planets shaped like eggs,
The asteroids like fish,
The diatom,
The giant, the more feeble stars,
And the innumerable nameless presences
Familiar to the Eye
Or in the hollow
Of the dark, reposing Hand.

V

The King o fairy with his rout
Com to hunt him all about
With dim cry and bloweing,
And houndes also with him berking.
Ac no best they no nome,
No never he nist wheder they bicome.

The Lay of Sir Orfeo,
anonymous, 13th century

What Would Make a Boy Think to Kill Bats?

I'd always thought I knew how bats caught bugs,
Big mouths opening spiked with rodent teeth,
But no, they scoop their prey up in midair
By cupping the web between hind legs and tail.
Watching them in slow motion made me think
How many nightfalls in the failing light,
How many nights in the succeeding shadow,
As a boy, I watched them browse and never saw
How for an instant with cupped wings and tail
They made their bodies into leather baskets,
Or how, in flight, they dipped their heads far in
To pluck the catch up out of the bottom,
Sometimes performing a somersault full tuck.

At twelve I found them—dozens draped heads down
Around the walls inside the dairy, sleeping.
Strange, I plucked them in their sleep with a BB gun.
Some had high-pitched barely audible screams
Which they made with jaws wide open. Others dropped
Without a sign. Why did I want them dead?

I remember the sight of them, how it was
Loathsome: lumps of dark flesh hanging from the wall,
Most of them rabid, I believed, things
Dangerous to have alive, and above all

Ugly, waking nightmares, although now,
When I remember the scene, as again
And again I do, the bats like warm-blooded angels
Unfold themselves with supple intricate wings,
With little cries of anguish, and no more
Can they frighten me, not now, not the bats.

Peaceable Kingdom

How many times did Edward Hicks paint
The Peaceable Kingdom? Seven score?
Can you imagine? Lamb and wolf,
Leopard with kid, lion, bull, and babe,
Like cherubim in Earthly Paradise,
While Penn's boys and the Indians made
Peace and Pennsylvania in the hills—
More than a hundred paintings, each
To be given a neighbor, a Friend,
As a token of faith, painting by painting,
Year after year, settlers west,
Treaty by treaty, settling the savage
Into that unimaginary land
Where lay the bison, the puma, and the wolf.

Economics

When it hatches awake in its dark cell,
A wasp with no confession of remorse
Eats of the trapdoor spider's living flesh
Which tolerates this, being paralyzed,
For torture never was unnatural,
Not even for the way, to do his job,
The torturer may cancel that one chance
Ever to have had a decent life:
When bees leave entrails dangling from a sting
To fall and writhe in such pain as bees know,
Their glory must be like a warrior's death,
Not that the boy stung cares more than to crush
Whatever's left of disemboweled bee.
Our economics of enlightened greed—
Tired of the pretext of enlightenment—
Works not unlike a dream worldwide, a dream
Impervious to the interpreter
Because it is so nakedly itself:
The severed testicles crammed into a daughter's mouth.

Glee

Coons manhandle corn—
Ten stalks down one morning,
Wasted, not a whole ear eaten.
What's a man to do?

Well, coon hunt is one thing,
And if you want to get out at night,
And hold a gun in your lap,
And hearken the belling of Catahoulas,
Blue ticks, and the rest,
Sipping it neat from a flask
While dew drops on your bootlace,
Then, coon hunt may be *the* thing.

Yet hounds at half a mile at midnight,
Haunting glisses and chords,
Reveal, in their elusive beauty, to me,
Nothing of use on a coon hunt
Or even worth mentioning in the woods.

And my poor, poor ignorant stray
Has proven among the pack of experts
Eager and useless as I.
She was the one

To follow the scent alone,
Whooping and yapping with glee.

"That must be your bitch," said Martin.

"Yeah? What do you think?" That unpropitious
Note of pride not hidden.

"Ain't none of mine.
She picked up a cat." He meant bobcat.

And she followed the scent in her frenzy
Farther into the hardwoods
Up the winding moonlit creek bed
On bright sand and gravel
Up the gulley bottom of clay
Into the dark brush
Giving tongue
On through briars and through green thorns
Till at a faint, faint distance
Her hysteria doubled.

"She seen him."

And she held that tempo
Into the pine hills

Up to the pasture
Where she doubled again.

"He'd be stopped now
And she gone to circling him."

Ah! That faithful stray still calling
Far off, calling me,
Fearless after mistaken prey
Until we heard her cry.

Hand and Foot

Dark woods, daybreak, coffee on the sagging porch, a blue-gray
    gnatcatcher alighted on my sleeve,
hopped down the seam, head swiveled, black beak opened, tongue—
    blade thin and trembling—arched,

no cry, no call, hopped to the naked skin inside my wrist, and—
    through scaled toe,
through talon, through piped legbone—touched me, quickened,
    flew, and I would find myself

years later, idling in a heap near dead under the light at 94th
    on Broadway,
and a woman, mannish with unwieldy knife, tore after someone,
    nobody, the good-for-nothing,

drunk the both of them, no longer young. Across the car she
    cursed and threatened, leaning,
left palm livid on the windshield near my face, night falling,
    and the light had changed.

Under the horns she waved us on, and I remembered the electric
    tarsus at my wrist,
as if it mattered, how in a burst of blues and brilliances the
    gnatcatcher took flight.

Not Wild or Mongolian Now,
nor Ever Truly an Ass

" . . . the only borough whose name is preceded by 'The'—The
Bronx, as though there could be another! The custom seems
to have survived from the days when the whole area was
known as 'The Broncks' Farm.' 'The' endured even though
'Farm' and the family for which it was named have vanished."
                    History Preserved, Goldstone and Dalrymple

The wild Mongolian ass lives
Only in The Bronx,
Corralled into a corner at the zoo
Where having read the sign I stood
Among the bypassers in awe
Of that dispirited flesh, their whole species
Standing together looking into the ground.
So I repeated aloud to myself their name—
Not theirs, of course, but only ours for them,
Or rather not for them, for us—
However it was, I read the name on the sign,
Wild Mongolian ass, and tried to imagine them
At a canter over the steppes
Or pausing to graze on a high slope in the Urals,
As though I knew how steppes or Urals looked,
And I wondered if, having been born in The Bronx,
They might be keeping in genetic code
The memory of ancestral wilderness,
To think of which I looked down at the ground,

I stared into the dust like them,
And I found nothing there,
Not awe, nor vestiges nor inklings
Even of understanding, only dust, a waiting ground
For the swift, the ancient transport they were due.

The Clarinet

How does the eucalyptus leaf taste
To the koala bear, soul-satisfying
Or so-so? Could the music of the spheres
Sound to the human ear the way brine
Feels to the grouper gill, the way the jungle
Upside down strikes the intelligence of a sloth?
Mark Twain put it in the Homeric question
This way: Did Homer write the *Iliad*
And the *Odyssey*, or was it a man who just
Called himself Homer? To have the cosmos
Making oblivious music all the time
Is hardly more absurd than to believe
That light at certain wavelengths can't be seen.
For how can it be light and not be seen?
Or music and nobody hear? It can't.
Can it? Remember how the clarinet
Found Mozart in its ecstasy. Watch light
Up in the dark crisscross among the stars.

Pond

When the water scalded in the shallows
and the mud closed on our anklebones
while sunken leaves gave up the gas
of their long rotting underwater,
in a cow pond, horse pond, full of the flop and urine,
we would swim even when August
raised steam rank as the ripening of a body.

After a dry spell when the clay red surface
sank in and the deeper green tinged
water oak and live oak leaves reflected,
when the torso of the cottonmouth behind the stob of head wedge
curved twice into the zero visibility of one foot under,
turtles tilted in their disks of darkness
in and out of sight,
the elegant slider with red earmarks, stinkpot, cooter.

Cat with wide head narrowing into body,
largemouth big as a newborn, bluegill, punkinseed,
the minnows everywhere, the tadpoles,
gnats in tall clouds, cruising dragonflies,
the damselflies adrift and horseflies circling,
skaters, striders, over the water scorpion's slow motion,
plunge of the diving beetle, giant waterbug (that prowler,
one-fanged, forelegs built to spring their deathtrap on a fingerling),

bullbats striking the double trail across still water with their
    wingtips—

into this the pack of us boys went splashing, laughing, shrieking
    curses,
down the bank where Zion's congregation
sanctified these waters with baptizing,
sang hymns, preached waist deep with white robe floating,
where in worship children of my mother's father's grandfather's
    slaves' children
still on that same bank stood witness, witnessed also
by jackmule, jenny, bull and steer,
mare and foal, and turkey buzzard miles up circling,
witnessed by the little bossman in the congregation,
witnessed fear struck in a child's eye when the large hand closed
on mouth and nose to pull her under.
"No!" the eye said,
but she went down backwards, bending backward at the knee,
the waist, resisting, stiff, she could not swim,
but gave herself into the preacher's hands,
she clutched his wrist, hands bound, was taken under,
and the congregation did not speak,
the preacher looked down at the surface,
and O Lord we saw where she was gone
into the mud cloud in the water. Gone.

Her mother wept. I wept. I did not know her.
Gone too long. Gone one whole second. And another
second. Second. And the congregation went down
in our souls we went down in broad daylight
where we could not breathe
we held ourselves too long
too long till she rose up again and all saw
she was shaken
O Lord
by the Power
all stood shaken by the Power
which with first breath broke among us
into the sung praises.

Down that same bank now in cut-offs, tearing into the water,
rousing cattle egret, killdeer, kingfisher,
and green and great blue heron,
watched by the indifferent mule and mallard,
by the suspicious goose, we
hedonists of twelve, of thirteen, fourteen, fifteen,
came to swim.

We the guilty children, smokers of cross vine, trumpet vine,
dried corn silk, coffee, smokers of the bad cigar shoplifted,
keepers of hidden knowledge,

we cult worshippers of forbidden pictures,
car thieves, kleptos, came, unbridled,
watched by draft horse, by beef cattle, watched
by nanny goat with two weeks' kid for our next Cajun cookout,
cut loose from our parents, came to swim,

where, Fafa warned us, one boy drowned when they were little,
died not understanding in the eighteen hundreds what occurred
was for the sake of stories to be told us lately
although none of us would drown or ever die
so that the boy's death had been truly pointless
which would ever be incomprehensible to elders
more so the more serious the Presbyterian
until the world was lost on deacons
such as he
who said interminable grace at breakfast.

So we listened
and tore straight down into the pond
where we would dive for bottom
where the dead boy was
my now dead grandfather's lost friend
inhabitant of the cold
that gave us gooseflesh even in the heat of August
keeper of the soft mud melting from the hand

before it made the surface
child mired where the oak limbs snap that dull snap
under the drone of engines worked into
and over the near country
under the hot world cold in an impenetrable darkness.

Notes

I

The bois d'arc (pronounced bo dock), also called the Osage orange, is a smallish tree with extremely hard wood, bright yellow under the bark. The frizzly chicken is a breed of good layers with strikingly disheveled plumage.

I I

"Justice": Greenville, Mississippi, has a higher percentage of Chinese than any other town its size or larger in this country, except San Francisco. Toward the end of the nineteenth century many Cantonese people came to the area as workers on the plantations, and by the 1920s they had opened nearly a hundred family-owned groceries, mostly on the edges of the black neighborhoods where they lived. When animosity between blacks and Chinese peaked early in the 1970s, there were several incidents of violence.

In "The Conversion Shift," any distortion of actual events is entirely justified by artistic considerations, if not by the lifelong dispensation of a youngest brother to make his elders squirm. Borrow pits or barrow pits (pronounced bargh, as in Edinburgh) are the sunken areas left where earth has been dug up for construction of the levees along the Mississippi River. Since barrow pits lie along the foot of the levee on the river side, they are flooded in the spring and many hold some water year-round.

I I I

"Leaving the Drugstore for Example" is a variation on a theme from Czeslaw Milosz's poem "Proof."

"Serenade Airborne": For documentation of the more or less random bombardment of civilians in Quang Ngai, the province bordering the Demilitarized Zone in Vietnam, see Jonathan Schell's *The Military Half.*

The painting of St. Francis in the museum of the Frick mansion in
New York City is by Giovanni Bellini.

"Anatomy": The governing idea, that any perceived entity is both a system
of smaller entities and a component in a system comprising a larger
entity, has come to this poem in good part from the writings of
Arthur Koestler. The image of the planet as a single cell comes from
Lewis Thomas. Part of "Soul" is a rephrasing of Einstein's equation $E = mc^2$.

IV

In the excerpt from the Book of Daniel, King Nebuchadnezzar promises
Daniel (whose Babylonian name is Belteshazzar) that Daniel will suffer
no punishment for the correct interpretation of Nebuchadnezzar's dream.
The dream foretells that Nebuchadnezzar will live seven years on all fours
among the beasts before he learns faith and regains his reason and his kingdom.

"Easter Mass for Little John": In section four, "the Shepherd's
vacant arms" are part of the constellation Boötes, where the arms
are not clearly defined by a pattern of stars. Section six is a variation on the
opening verses of the Gospel According to John. In section twelve, the
Sisters of the Summer Triangle are supernatural beings envisioned as the
personages for whom the constellations in the Summer Triangle are attributes.

V

The excerpt from *Sir Orfeo* relates to the time after Orfeo loses
Herodis, when he leaves his kingdom for the wilderness and lives ten years
and more among the beasts. The following is a paraphrase in Modern English:

> The King of Fairy with his troop
> Came to hunt where Orfeo was

With dim cry and blowing of horns
And also with hounds barking.
But they took not one beast
Nor did he ever know where they went.

In "Glee," the Catahoula hog dog is a hound somewhat resembling
the blue tick hound. Catahoulas with glass eyes, that is with
blue irises, are particularly valuable for their reputedly greater
intelligence, and may fetch several thousand dollars.

A NOTE ABOUT THE AUTHOR

BROOKS HAXTON, born in 1950, in Greenville, Mississippi, lived there until he left to study at Beloit College in Wisconsin, in 1968. Since then he has lived, working at various jobs, in Minneapolis, London, Natchez, Rome, Boston, New York City, Syracuse, and Washington, D.C. He has taught creative writing at George Mason University and the University of Maryland, and now teaches at Sarah Lawrence College. His honors include a university fellowship for two years at the Syracuse University Graduate Writing Program, a fellowship in poetry at the Wesleyan Writers Conference, mention as a finalist for the Walt Whitman Award, and grants-in-aid from the D.C. Commission on the Arts and the Ingram Merrill Foundation. His first book was a narrative poem, *The Lay of Eleanor and Irene*, published in 1985.

A NOTE ON THE TYPE

The text of this book was set in Centaur, the only type face designed by Bruce Rogers, the well-known American book designer. A celebrated penman, Rogers based his design on the roman face cut by Nicolas Jenson in 1470 for his Eusebius. Jenson's roman surpassed all of its forerunners and even today, in modern re-cuttings, remains one of the most popular and attractive of all type faces.

The italic used to accompany Centaur is Arrighi, designed by another American, Frederic Warde, and based on a Chancery face used by Lodovico degli Arrighi in 1524.

Composed, printed and bound by
Heritage Printers, Inc.
Charlotte, North Carolina

Designed by Cecily Dunham